the burgeoning world

Poems by
Sonja Johanson

GLASS LYRE PRESS

Copyright © 2020 Sonja Johanson
Paperback ISBN: 978-1-941783-69-6

All rights reserved: Except for the purpose of quoting brief passages for review, no part of this book may be reproduced or transmitted in any form or by any means, electronic or mechanical, including photocopying, recording, or by any information storage and retrieval system, without permission in writing from the publisher.

Design & Layout: Steven Asmussen
Cover Art: © Kondou | Dreamstime.com
Copyediting: Linda E. Kim

Glass Lyre Press, LLC
P.O. Box 2693
Glenview, IL 60025
www.GlassLyrePress.com

the burgeoning world

Contents

Invocation	1
Birds of America	2
A Spear of Sanctified Hyssop	3
Spell for Putting the Shape of a Wife in the Wall	4
Birkebeiners	5
Cassandra	6
Hills Wink	8
Some Trees [are nonbinary]	9
Descending from a Ferocious Intention	10
Polygonatum	11
Spell for a Child Afraid of Spiders	12
Spell for Smoking the Bees	13
demolition	14
Practicing in Snowshoes	15
Yellow Quilt	16
Three Deer in Oquossoc	17
Vrikshasana	18
Osage Oranges at the Arnold	19
Night Poem	20
murmuration	21
empathy of Trees, Malaga	22
Paddling Canals where the Colorado Ends	23
time to call a halt	24
Notes	25
Acknowledgments	26
About the Author	27

Invocation

Poet of the urban landscape —
I don't have a present to offer in return.

Poet of the urban landscape,
everything in my life really doesn't matter —
I don't have a present to offer in return.

Poet of the urban landscape,
make our cities livable, humane, inspiring.
Everything in my life really doesn't matter;
it means breath, air, climate, wind.
I don't have a present to offer in return.

Poet of the urban landscape —
a landscape that bears the marks of both —
make our cities livable, humane, inspiring.
Being in a place where I feel so small,
everything in my life really doesn't matter.
This combination of density and unstraight lines,
it means breath, air, climate, wind.
They are all valid; they all exist at the same time.
I don't have a present to offer in return.

Poet of the urban landscape —
green and ungridded,
a landscape that bears the marks of both —
it is its own wilderness.
Make our cities livable, humane, inspiring,
their practicality and resilience.
Being in a place where I feel so small,
seven storylines that end up intersecting,
everything in my own life really doesn't matter.
This adder, concealed within its green bosom,
this combination of density and unstraight lines,
they have to learn to listen to each other.
It means breath, air, climate, wind,
a memory from childhood of the missiles on their launches.
They are all valid; they all exist at the same time.
The thing from which everything goes and comes back —
I don't have a present to offer in return.

Birds of America

Lady Hertford had the tea room walls
in Temple Newsom House covered
with Chinese paper given her by the Prince
of Wales. A garden wrapped around that room —
gilt flowers, butterflies, graceful branches,
exotic birds. But not enough. Lady Hertford
wanted more. Arthritic fingers fussy-cut
Columbia jays, brown thrashers, swallow-tailed
hawks. She pasted orioles in the pear trees,
belted kingfishers over the joins.

This was before we knew the book
would be worth millions. Before we saw
the swift decline of Carolina parakeets.
We purchased cabinets for the tea service,
lacquered black with toxic sap. Before
we knew not to mix birds from one continent
and another, not to bring rabbits to Australia,
that tree lobsters slept with jointed limbs
wrapped gently around their mates, but ships rats
would wipe them out in two quick years.

This is the time we look back to —
this was the time of everything. Lord God
birds kinted in the swamps, heath hens
whirred and boomed on their leks,
botanists scoured the cloud forests,
bringing back *Maxillaria* orchids
for our glass houses. Maids set out
cups and saucers, sugar cubes and silver.

Darwin observed the shrike storing its victims,
the parasitoid wasp laying her eggs
in the living bodies of *Lepidoptera* larvae
and questioned the intent of God.

A Spear of Sanctified Hyssop

A frugal year could lift you
through the crown of your hat.

You would be willing to stand
discipline, you would lavish

charity on the wrong men, point
thoughtfully at the flask when

whiskey made them open up.
Well or ill, you would lie like

a pickpocket, sing like a rain-
crow clanking a copper-bell.

With your meditative cast of mind,
you would not need anything

so coarse and selfish as a world.

Spell for Putting the Shape of a Wife in the Wall

The wife is a bird, is a wishbone, is broken when you wish her to be. The bird is a cage, is a memory, is a time when you made yourself small enough to fit inside. The cage is a girdle of ribs, is a heartbeat, is the sleeping before the waking before the sleeping. The girdle is your hands around her waist, around her throat, pinkie to pinkie, thumb to thumb. Your hands are spiders, they unravel oranges, they furrow the soil. The spiders are somewhere, in the plaster and lathe, in the stairwell. Somewhere is a wall, is an outline, the pinnae, the feathers, somewhere is a cage, is memory and you are sleeping under her wing.

Birkebeiners

Tinker tells
us what we mostly know —
they should have kept
the firs,

the tree wells,
those boughs retaining snow.
Instead, they ripped
the earth,

tore out
anything that wasn't white.
Battle-mad, they rogued
the glade,

heedless
of the cost. Now, against a copse
of broken birch, we bark
our shins.

Cassandra

A juvenile humpback dies on Puget Sound.
Species evolve by chance mutations
and catastrophic events. Changes happen

by failure and deaths, a scale too small and large
for seeing. It takes years for a giant to die.
Arborists advise against the word suddenly.

Homeowners call to ask what killed their tree.
There is no "suddenly", we tell them.
The town regraded the road eight years ago.

Salt from the icy surface poured into cut roots
and now your *Cercus* fails to break its red buds.
This third year of drought, my *Liriodendron*

drops yellow leaves all summer, a monster
that will crush our house when it falls.
Mindful of the bills, I capture gray water,

milk the dehumidifier, set buckets under
the air conditioning, pouring shower water,
which sluiced down my body, under its spread.

Whale milk is cottage cheese thick,
a hundred gallons a day for a growing calf,
more when it turns to krill and fish, more

when the mysticetes open great mouths
to strain the seas. It takes a mountain
of empty water to starve a whale.

A rostrum rests against the science center —
ship strike, noise pollution, net entanglement,
the things we do to them. Across the campus

the radio told us cruise missiles were sent
to Iraq. We felt the ripples of the buildings
yet to fall, and shivered.

We studied quaternary extinction.
Even if you don't drive a herd of camels
off a cliff, or slaughter all the stag-moose,

even if you take only the mammoth
you need, and the next year the same,
one day there are no more mammoths.

So we love our last leviathans. We name
those big-winged rorquals, migrating
north to south, circumpolar, in every ocean.

We know them by their flukes, each tip and notch,
each trailing edge, each scar and rope burn.
We keep a catalogue, a photo album —

Trident, Anchor, Thalassa, Echo,
Apex and Eden, Compass and Fulcrum.
A juvenile dies on Puget Sound, starved.

I name her for the woman who saw the end —
who wailed and pulled her hair, who gnashed
her baleen teeth while no one listened.

Hills Wink

This. This first day in a year
of miracles, a year of words
falling from the fingertips,

energy falling off the body. Sun
plays; the space between trees,
each hickory a candle, lit or unlit,

each candle a day, a colour,
words which spiral through
weeks into months. Fires

blaze through icicles, crows
covet the shine. Hills wink;
even the hunting dog cares.

Some Trees [are nonbinary]

We choose some [*Gingko biloba*] only
to be male — tall, straight, shafted. Females

find their way, stinking ovules dropping
in the street grates. Even the males chichi;

buds swell into gender-defying pendulosities.
Some [*Ilex verticillata*] demand big love,

and who are you to judge them?
Southern gentlemen courting as many

winter red ladies as the wind allows.
Other trees [*Alnus glutinosa*] flaunt it

both ways. Staminate catkins swing,
long and thick. On the same branches

pistils open their green lips, receptive.
Most trees [*Prunus virginiana*] never leave

the bedroom — the way they touch themselves,
cleistogamous. We call these flowers *perfect*.

Descending from a Ferocious Intention

There is no way to say
how much I need those words —

I write them everywhere, press
the rough bark of them across

my skin, score them in my forearm —
a cutting, an unmasking.

I paint myself to blinding, carve
it in calligraphy and no one

has to ask me what it means.
They know. These words

thrown in my father's face, once
for every time my mother told me

that I should have been a boy.
These are my pepper spray, my mace,

rape-whistling in the ears
of men who mistook me

for a blossom. These are the shears
I took to my own locks, me

my own Delilah (is hair the source
of sex, is sex the source of strength,

if I had something else to cut
would I have done it, if I had some

other power would I choose it?)
These are the words to tell you

I am not the pinkness or
the weeping — I am the graft.

There is this thing that eats the sun;
I am the thing that keeps it down.

Polygonatum

slip under the soil
pale knobby root thing
crooked rhizome sealed with scars

nothing to anyone else

be buried
be somewhere shaded

quiet empty place damp
liminal place for weeds
creeping out the woods

only another shoot
in the burgeoning world

break the shell of the earth
green egg tooth pierce the day

rise and unwrap

axil
deep ribs
alternating leaf
parallel veins

hanging white
the odor of memory

Spell for a Child Afraid of Spiders

It was never like they told you. There were no wolves in the nursery, there was nothing waiting to kiss you in your sleep. There were only book lungs gently breathing, the sway of silk pulled into air, a mother who carried her children closer to her body. There were only two-part guardians, and they watched you from their corners, shadow eyes and ocelli awake. They never brushed you with their pedipalps, they never bit, they loved you like a changeling, they draped the walls with curtains, they quieted your rest. These, these are your own, these are your parents, open your hand and let them take you home.

Spell for Smoking the Bees

Use any fuel — punky floorboards, green pine needles, rags soaked in skunky beer — anything to smoulder. State by state we'll vote it in, faster than assisted suicide. Thuribles swung in church, referenda passed, censer filled with frankincense and myrrh. The living blood of Christ, of trees, sap, resin, amber, insects trapped inside forever. Smoke to mask alarm, make us forget, to make us hungry, we fill up on honey never noticing the hive. The deal between insect and flower, the way plants bypass it, choose to grow in sealed houses, choose to clone instead of mixing genes. We'll leave behind the battles, beatings, pheromones telling us warning, warning, bear claws rending us open, aliens lifting our roofs to steal our children. We'll take in the sweet scent, the wax warming, we'll move our eyes beneath our lids to see the danger for the dream it really is.

demolition

it should be   some comfort
    that history
        has come to you   by accident

  branches   tapping the window
       fear   hunger   work
you did not earn it
        the house
              now gone
  the angry man   the closet
                for hiding

nor
   did you deserve it   as you do not
               deserve   the rain in winter
      the dim gray sun   or dry cave

   it is only   what you were born to
      so take it   unblinking
          say its name

remember
           that you walk   this path
because this   is the way
         things happen
    in the world

Practicing in Snowshoes

Focus your gaze
      on fur rippling
around your vision

      Heels press down
ovals of ash-splint
      sinew underfoot

Mittens, boiled wool
      caked in white crust
fingertips burning —

      Stone chapel, closed
c'est l'eglise
      the arched red door

Look up; snowflakes —
      they drift in,
settle on your boots

Yellow Quilt

It rains, cold rain. When you are gone
I slip into
lake water, full
of lavender

and lemon balm, warm and drawn to
a blessed bath.
With your hands, it
strokes my shoulders,

the nape of my knees. Your scent still
lingers on the
rumpled covers —
sweetfern and gale.

Three Deer in Oquossoc

East will take me back.
I drive west. I wend
between snowbanks,
until the road delivers me
to a sleeping boat launch.

They stand on the frozen ramp;
watch me with coats that are
better than mine. Snowmobiles
and ice houses edge the distance.
I have to turn around, I say,
I went the wrong way.
They stamp and chuff. *No,*
they tell me, *this is the way.*

Vrikshasana

This —
my body
to your body,
skin to bark, flesh
becomes sapwood,
heartwood, spleen.

Respiration.
Your breath in, my breath
out. You transpire, stomata
open, mouths, nostrils
gasping. I die a little.

Branches, brachia, arms,
axillary buds burst —
watersprouts. I reach.

We both turn to the sun,
my face, your lamina.
Sweet, sweet sugar.
We drink it in.
We send it down.

Messages in the soil,
hyphael exchanges;
we speak in chemical
whispers, root to root,
rustle to
rustle.

Osage Oranges at the Arnold

A garden, yes, but also
a haven for lovers,
addicts, joggers
and other lost souls
choking to death
on the city

A tree museum
where we are curating
species we are wiping out
beside species we are bringing in
to kill them

Forbidden, yes
but not the fruit of knowledge
only a hedge apple
long divorced
from its seed disperser, whispering
where are the mammoths? and
how did I get here?

Snakes, torpid now,
even the images
carved into this skin
a frieze full of miniscule elvers,
a green brain moving,
heavy in the hand —
the weighty sin
of stealing them

Night Poem

        I cannot say anything
is a miracle

Words are born at an empty table
        in an empty house
and only when we are listening
                for other things:

prehistoric growling of a freight train

click of a stopwatch button

a loon seeking company across the pond

      from that moment on
               every sound
         a marvel

water is never wasted —
   whatever runs off the hydrophobic soil
        gets taken up

     boat in the cove of your shoulder
      I rock

somewhere else
it rains

murmuration

I care, about the language, the shape
vowels take, slipping from your tongue,

obsidian, sleek, volcanic: the way you see
my words written as I speak them to you:

insistent buzzing of your voice behind
my ears as I read your hand: our breath

breezing out the window: flocks of starlings
passing, wheeling: apart, together, apart, up.

empathy of Trees, Malaga

living so precariously, so easily
undermined by insistence

of water, geometry of swells,
frequencies which could lift

a saltbox as easily as a boat,
fog that would hide the banks

for days, still you loved that spare
island, the barnacled rocks were

as your heart, fish your children,
dark-skinned oaks your company.

Why should these have been taken from you?

Paddling Canals where the Colorado Ends

                                              half-empty glass
you have poured yourself to nothing
where marriage goes to die

                          salt-plain and tamarisk
              tiny streams should be draining here
into a wet meadow

now burning waste water
almost reaches a finger of the sea

if I stretched out my hand
                            would it raise a tidal bore
                   would it empty reservoirs

              everything we've held back
copepods waking
      ecological memory

        willow switches rooting
                  in the sand

would the dendrite — great tree —
        etched across the plain

                        become a living river

    lush delta
turning green again when we thought it
              lost for good

time to call a halt

watermelons
booming up
into the sun

sunflower and sage
unpolluted by dust
no guile about them

carefreeness wobble-
kneed as blue foxgloves
vast and blinding

how much wealthier
they were on the shirt-
tail end of nothing

Notes

Pg. 1 Oulipo constraint, larding. All text selected from the *Boston Globe*, April 25, 2014

Pg. 3 Pastiche, source text H.L. Davis's novel *Honey in the Horn*, 1935

Pg. 8 after Spencer Finch's installation commemorating Dickinson's Miraculous Year. http://www.mymodernmet.com/profiles/blogs/spencer-finch-366-emily-dickinson-s-miraculous-year

Pg. 9 after John Ashbery's "Some Trees"

Pg. 10 Title taken from Mark Doty's poem "Amagansett Cherry"

Pg. 22 after Daniel Minter's painting "empathy of Trees"

Pg. 24 Pastiche, source text H.L. Davis's novel "Honey in the Horn", 1935

Acknowledgments

Thanks to the following journals for giving these poems their first homes:

Avocet: "Hills Wink"
Bad Pony: "Spell for Smoking the Bees"
concis: "Practicing in Snowshoes"
Cream City Review: "Birds of America", "Night Poem"
Dunes Review: "Osage Oranges at the Arnold", "Paddling where the Colorado Ends"
Erstwhile: "time to call a halt"
Mid-American Review: "Spell for a Child Afraid of Spiders"
Ninth Letter: "Cassandra"
Outlook Springs: "Polygonatum", "demolition"
Plum Tree Tavern: "empathy of Trees, Malaga", "Three Deer in Oquossoc"
Poet Lore: "Spell for Putting the Shape of a Wife in the Wall"
Porkbelly Press: "Some trees [are nonbinary]", "Descending from a Ferocious Intention"
Port Yonder Press: "Spear of Sanctified Hyssop", "Vrikasana"
Still: The Journal: "murmuration"
White Stag: "Invocation"

About the Author

Sonja Johanson holds an MFA in poetry from the Warren Wilson Program for Writers, and has recent work appearing in *American Life in Poetry*, *Cincinnati Review*, and *Sugar House Review*. Her most recent chapbook is *Trees in Our Dooryards* (Redbird Chapbooks). Sonja divides her time between work in Massachusetts and her home in the mountains of western Maine. Follow her at www.sonjajohanson.net.

Glass Lyre Press

exceptional works to replenish the spirit

Glass Lyre Press is an independent literary publisher interested in technically accomplished, stylistically distinct, and original work. Glass Lyre seeks diverse writers that possess a dynamic aesthetic and an ability to emotionally and intellectually engage a wide audience of readers.

Glass Lyre's vision is to connect the world through language and art. We hope to expand the scope of poetry and short fiction for the general reader through exceptionally well-written books, which evoke emotion, provide insight, and resonate with the human spirit.

Poetry Collections
Poetry Chapbooks
Select Short & Flash Fiction
Anthologies

www.GlassLyrePress.com

www.ingramcontent.com/pod-product-compliance
Lightning Source LLC
Chambersburg PA
CBHW030142100526
44592CB00011B/1012